HEARTBEAT *of an* APOSTLE

Revelation From The Heart Of Paul

Dr. John Polis

HEARTBEAT OF AN APOSTLE
Revelation From The Heart Of Paul
By John Polis

PAPERBACK ISBN: 978-1-7377236-5-3
Also available for Hardback and ebook

Prepared for Publication By

MAKING YOUR BOOK A REALITY

Cedar Point, NC | 843-929-8768 | info@BandBpublishingLLC.com

John Polis Ministries
600 The Drive
Fairmont, WV 26554
www.johnpolis.com

Printed in the United States of America.

CONTENTS

Foreword

BY SAMUEL POLIS

It's early in 1850, a woman holds under her cloak a bulky object, trying at all costs to keep it out of sight from the Inspectors as she travels back to her home country of Poland. Although the trip has the usual trials associated with travel, it is the deathbed promise made to her brother that weighs upon her most and surpasses any fears or obstacles that arise. Finally the Church of the Holy Cross in Warsaw looms in front, and she takes out the object and hands it over to be secreted beneath a small monument within. The task completed, she fades from history, but the act she has performed, a deed of love and virtue, is timeless. Under the monument, where no eye can see, lies a heart...floating in a murky amber fluid, a heart now still, but that once composed some of the greatest notes as it beat, the heart of the inimitable composer Chopin is finally at home in his beloved

Poland as he had made his sister promise. The words written on the small monument? They are eternal words, spoken by the Christ and recorded in the book of Matthew; "Where your treasure is, there will your heart be also."

No words ring more true, and no persons having read the letters written by the Apostle Paul to those that he labored for, could avoid the constant sense of his heartbeat, the cadence of his life that with almost an uncanny rhythm pervades every word he writes. They linger on the pages like notes on a musical chart, with unseen time signatures that as they are read, bring an order to the life of the Christ follower.

Like all of us, Paul had to live with his former self, and the memories of all he had persecuted and destroyed, Yet his letters hold no detailed references to those memories, he doesn't bother to burden the reader with a weight that he himself has chosen to cast off. This in and of itself is an indication of Pauls great heart, and how he chose to serve the cause of Christ. Pauls treasure, his tireless heartbeat, was to see every Christ follower completely renewed, with no allegiance to a darkened past. Instead he leads us to a glorious light, the same one that once left him horseless and blind, to a mirror that is no longer unclear, but instead reveals the image of Christ as we gaze within.

In every letter, every word that he squeezed from his heart leads us to a finish line, his own past shrugged daily, no matter the hardship. Paul's heartbeat was one of courage, knowing that the opposite of courage is not cowardice, it's conformity. He reveals with every beat how he has accepted the new man, and would not, regardless of the very real fears in his life, conform to an old one. Paul knows it is hard, he defaults to military rhetoric when describing the trials, and to what type of soldier one must be. The author G. K. Chesterton summarized it definitively when he said, "The Christian ideal has not been tried and found wanting. It has been found difficult and left untried." Pauls heartbeat was to leave all of us with a clear view of the finish line, and the wisdom needed to run towards it sans any baggage we may have acquired in life.

Paul left his heart intertwined in his words, and the beat still felt as we read them...the great treasure of his life, that crown that was laid before him in heavens beyond, a crown of Righteousness, not just for him as he constantly reminds, but for all who have loved Christs appearing. (2 Timothy 4:8)

Chapter One

THE MISSIONARY HEART

"I am a debtor both to Greeks and to barbarians, both to wise and to unwise. So, as much as is in me, I am ready to preach the gospel to you who are at Rome also. For I am not ashamed of the gospel of Christ, for it is the power of God to salvation for everyone who believes, for the Jew first and also to the Greek." Romans 1:14-16 NKJV

Paul reveals his heart to reach all people with the gospel of Christ and gives three reasons why he will do so.

I AM A DEBTOR.

Here is the reason why all Christians should have a measure of the apostolic heart after having been impacted by the ministry anointing of an apostle. Apostles will impart to us a "sense of obligation," as Paul says, "I am a DEBTOR." When the apostolic heart has been revealed to us, we also will sense our obligation to share the good news with others, we will all become missionaries to the part of this world God has called us to live in and influence. Many Christians have no sense of obligation at all regarding the responsibility we have to share what we know about Jesus Christ with others. I remember my attitude to my debts before I was born again, I oftentimes would let them go to collection with the intention of never paying them at all. I was a "taker" and not a "giver" who lived for self exclusively, not unlike many others without Christ. But when I was saved, what a change came into my life regarding my obligations, I make sure all my bills are paid on time and that I have an excellent credit rating. I became conscientious about my debts in the natural and in the spiritual realm, I want to have a good name as a Christian.

I attended Dayton Bible College in the late '70's in Dayton, Ohio where I obtained a B.A. in Biblical Studies. One of our courses was on the major cults with at textbook by Jack Sparks. He made a comment that has never left me, he said, "The cults are the unpaid bills of the church." God impacted me with this saying as I realized that Jesus had paid my "debts," all the sins I had committed and ever would commit, but he also left me with a debt to pay. My debts include all the lost people of this world, I owe it to Jesus to tell them about what He has done for all of us. I also owe it to them because I "know the truth" regarding Eternal Life, and for me to withhold a lifesaving device from a drowning person would be criminal. The church today that lives in the "me culture," may never give thought to the obligation we all have to spread the good news of Jesus Christ. The excuses range from, "that's not my spiritual gift" to, "I don't have that kind of personality." But when our hearts are touched with the apostolic grace, we will realize that the "love of God has been shed abroad in our hearts" resulting in a great sense of obligation for the eternal destiny of others.

I remember hearing Oral Robert tell a story at the World Conference of Morris Cerullo Ministries in Anaheim, California back in the late '80's. He called it "Please Pass The Butter" and it went as follows.

"There was as certain family sitting around the dinner table at Christmas time enjoying the long awaited holiday feast, they were discussing the gifts they had received under the tree. One young girl commented on the Tape Recording machine she had received and decided to record the conversation around the table by all the visiting relatives. As the meal progressed and everyone shared with enthusiasm, all of a sudden a small boy shouted at the top of his lungs, 'PLEASE PASS THE BUTTER'. His father scolded him for the rude manners and sent him off to his room without dinner where he was to reflect on how to behave at table. After dinner, all were relaxing in the living room when the young girl suggested that they all listen to the recording from the dinner table. As they listened, they heard a faint voice saying in normal tone, 'please pass the butter'. A little later in the conversation they heard the same voice only this time a little louder and irritated, "please pass the butter'. Finally as the tape continued, they heard the shout from the young boy that got him in trouble saying 'PLEASE PASS THE BUTTER'. Then they all realized that the young boy had been trying to get someone's attention to pass the butter, but all were too busy in their own conversations to pay attention to the need of this boy. So, he was punished unjustly and everyone apologized for not being more sensitive, especially Dad." The point of the story is this, people are all around us saying, "Please pass the butter," are we hearing them? We may not recognize the cry for help in their eye or voice as they share the problem or need they face at the moment, but they are really asking us to share what we have with them. Let us "pass the butter."

I AM READY.

Paul goes on to reveal the impact of this "sense of obligation" upon his own life by indicating how he had prepared himself in response. He says, "as much as is in, I am READY." Wow! No half hearted effort here, "as much as is in me" means he gave it a 110% effort. In other words, "I have done all to prepare myself to meet the challenges of sharing the gospel in any culture and to any ethnic group." This is the "missionary heart." Why do we "go to church," "attend bible studies and conferences" if not to prepare ourselves to share the gospel effectively. Without the "sense of obligation," we will study and learn all we can just to enhance our own lives and live the dream of prosperity that we believe God wants us to enjoy. We must lift our vision to the whitened harvest fields and be "prepared to give an answer for the hope that is in our hearts." God is waiting for the church to bring in the harvest of the "former and latter rains" so that He can send His Son back to this earth (James 5:7-8). Paul urged Timothy to be fully prepared to share his faith by being a diligent student of the Word.

> *"Be diligent to present yourself approved to God, a worker who does not need to be ashamed, rightly dividing the word of Truth." 2 Timothy 2:15 NKJV*

Paul was prepared with the "wisdom and revelation" of the Word of God, he was ready to explain the "finished work of Christ" in enough detail to convince the unbelievers of their need to receive Jesus as Lord. It is sad to say that most cults today have gleaned their members from former Christian church attendees or members who never applied themselves to study the Bible and were able to be seduced from the faith with "doctrines of demons" (1 Timothy 4:1). Have you studied what "you" believe, and what the "other guy" believes as well so that you can show them the difference in truth and error? When we have become "debtors," we will also get "ready."

I AM NOT ASHAMED.

Finally, Paul says what he knows about the gospel of Christ, "it is the power of God." Paul knows and expects that the power of God will manifest as he preaches the gospel so that the message will be confirmed and people will be without excuse. Have you ever had the urge to share the gospel with someone but balked because you would be ashamed if God suddenly showed up and "caused a scene." Maybe the person will begin to cry, or worse yet, maybe they will want you to pray for them and others are nearby and might hear you. How about this, what if you prayed for them and they were slain by the power of God right there in the parking lot? Paul was ready for anything and was not ashamed to be "identified" with Christ who would show up and show out. We see an example from Paul's ministry in Lystra where he was stoned for manifesting the power of the gospel.

> *"And in Lystra a certain man without strength in his feet was sitting, a cripple from his mother's womb, who had never walked. This man heard Paul speaking. Paul observed him intently and seeing that he had faith to be healed, said with a loud voice, "Stand up straight on your feet!" And he leaped and walked." Acts 14:8-9 NKJV*

The crowd got so excited that they began to proclaim that Paul and Barnabas were Greek gods and they wanted to sacrifice to them. Paul stopped them from trying to worship them as "mere men," but the word got out regarding this miracle and Jews from Antioch and Iconium came and stoned Paul, and supposing that he was dead, dragged him out of the city. I like the next verse,

> *"However, when the disciples gathered around him, he rose up and went into the city. And the next day he departed with Barnabas to Derbe." Acts 14:19 NKJV*

The same Spirit that raised Christ from the dead lived in

Paul and raised him up in complete health so that he could go right back to his apostolic assignment without interruption. This same "missionary heart" of the apostle can be our heart as well. Pray and ask the Father,

Give me the missionary heart that has a sense of my obligation to share the good news, the dedication to prepare myself as a workman and the courage to identify with Christ and His power, In Jesus Name. Amen.

Chapter Two

THE THANKFUL HEART

> *"And I thank Christ Jesus our Lord who has enabled me, because He counted me faithful, putting me into the ministry, although I was formerly a blasphemer, a persecutor, and an insolent man; but I obtained mercy because I did it ignorantly in unbelief. And the grace of our Lord was exceedingly abundant, with faith and love which are in Christ Jesus." 1 Timothy 1:12-14 NKJV*

In this expression from the "heart of Paul," we can sense how deeply grateful he was to have the privilege to serve Jesus Christ since he at one time tried to eradicate His Name from the earth. He describes himself as a "blasphemer, persecutor and insolent man" and fully realizes that it is only by the mercy of God that he was given a place in the service of the King. The Book of Acts records how vehemently he sought out followers of Christ to imprison and kill them.

> *"Then Saul, still breathing threats and murder against the disciples of the Lord, went to the High Priest and asked letters from him to the synagogues of Damascus, so that if he found any who were of the Way, whether men or women, he might bring them bound to Jerusalem." Acts 9:1-2 NKJV*

If we understand the truth about our own condition before salvation, we would know that we also were "enemies of Christ" who were at war with His purposes. Paul, writing to the Romans, tells us of our fourfold condition before coming to know Christ as Savior. Even though we may not have been the "religious zealot" that Paul was, openly at war with Christianity, yet in our hearts sin was at war against the Love of God.

> *"For when we were still without strength, in due time Christ died for the ungodly. For scarcely for a righteous man will one die; yet perhaps for a good man someone would even dare to die. But God demonstrates His own love toward us, in that while we were yet sinners, Christ died for us. Much more then, having now been justified by His blood, we shall be saved from wrath through Him. For if when we were enemies we were reconciled to God through the death of His*

> *Son, much more, having been reconciled, we shall be saved by His life. Romans 5:6-10 NKJV*

We were:

- ***Without strength*** - incapable of fulfilling His moral laws.
- ***Ungodly*** - the opposite of what He is.
- ***Sinners*** - those practicing sin as a lifestyle.
- ***Enemies*** - people at war with God and His purposes.

A good friend of mine, Rev. Frank Shaw who has gone to Heaven, a former teacher at Faith School of Theology in Bangor, Maine, once impacted me with this powerful statement, he said, "*John, you can't get someone saved, until you first get them lost.*" Paul the apostle knew how "lost" he was before Christ came into his life, and the thought that Jesus would give him an "apostleship" was almost more than he could describe. He knew how desperately he needed salvation in order to change the person that he was and transform him into the "image of God" once again. It concerns me that so often we invite people to accept Jesus for all the wrong reasons, which results in very little gratitude in the hearts of some professing Christians. We tell them, "just accept Jesus and he will fix your problems," or "get saved and live the abundant life, God wants you to prosper and be in health." These things are true enough but are not the basis for a life of gratitude to God for saving us from "His wrath." I agree with Rev. Shaw, "we must get them lost before we get them saved." People must have a revelation of what God has "saved them from" in terms of their spiritual condition. Paul was explicit in letting the Ephesians know what their condition was without Christ.

> *"And you He made alive, who were dead in trespasses and sins, in which you once walked according to the course of this world, according to the prince of the power of the air, the spirit who now works in the sons of disobedience, among whom also we all once conducted ourselves in the lusts of our flesh, fulfilling the desires of the flesh and of the mind, and were by nature children of wrath, just as the others. But God, who is rich in mercy, because of His great love with which He loved us, even when we were dead in trespasses, made us alive together with Christ (by grace you have been saved)." Ephesians 2:1-5 NKJV*

This kind of knowledge will make for a grateful heart, overflowing with good works and service to the King who has rescued us from ourselves and the wrath to come by His great love. Jesus tells of a woman how continually "kissed his feet" out of the overflow of a grateful heart due to His mercy in her life.

> *"Then he turned to the woman and to Simon, "Do you see this woman? I entered your house; you gave Me no water for My feet, but she has washed My feet with her tears and wiped them*

with the hair of her head. You gave Me no kiss, but this woman has not ceased to kiss My feet since the time I came in. You did not anoint My head with oil, but this woman has anointed My feet with fragrant Oil. Therefore I say to you, her sins, which are many, are forgiven, for she loved much. But to whom little is forgiven, the same loves little. Luke 7:44-47 NKJV

I expect this is the kind of gratitude Paul had in his heart for Jesus as well, knowing that he had "sinned much" and was forgiven of all. This principle will produce the most ardent workers of the Cross who totally abandon themselves to the Christ Life, to live as He lived, and for what He lived. We need this kind of grateful heart in the church of Christ today, and it will come as people understand just how great His mercy is toward us all. All true apostles have this understanding and the thankfulness that results.

Paul gives three reasons for his "thankfulness" to Christ Jesus in this passage of scripture.

1. "WHO HAS ENABLED ME."

The greek word is "endunamoo," meaning "to empower." Paul was well aware of the spiritual gift he received when he was filled with the Spirit of God. Paul knew that anything accomplished of eternal value was the result of the power of Holy Spirit at work in his life, God's abundant grace. We must all realize what a great gift we have received from the Lord Jesus in the infilling of the Spirit. The mighty Third Person of the Godhead has come to reside in us, and as someone has aptly stated, "We must make Him President, not just Resident." The key to greater power being manifested by Holy Spirit is our surrender to Him as Lord in our daily life (2 Corinthians 4:17). An intimate walk with Holy Spirit is the result of being.

- ***FILLED WITH THE SPIRIT*** - "and they were all filled with the Spirit and spoke with tongues." Acts 2:1-4; Acts 10:44-48; Acts 19:1-11

- ***FELLOWSHIP WITH THE SPIRIT*** - "And do not grieve the Holy Spirit of God, by whom you were sealed for the day of redemption." Ephesians 4:29-32

- ***FLOW WITH THE SPIRIT*** - "Out of your belly shall flow rivers of living water." John 7:37-38

Being grateful for the Gift of the Holy Spirit in our lives will cause us to be sensitive to Him at all times by learning His attributes and allowing them to be manifested in our lives. He is "kind, tenderhearted and forgiving" (Ephesians 4:32). I remember a life changing encounter I had with Holy Spirit, while teaching a class on the "Authority of the Believer" in Asheville, NC some years ago. I was telling the students that Jesus cast out demons with "authority and power (Luke 4:36), and that just having "authority in Christ" was not sufficient to bring deliverance, but that we also needed His power or anointing to cast out demons. While I was speaking, I saw the Holy Spirit through the "gift of discerning of spirits," I saw His form and was staggered by the look on His face. He looked as though he was skeptical of me and was keeping His distance. Then He spoke to me and said, "I would like to enfold you with my power, but when I seek to draw near to you, you "hurt me by being unkind to people." I was broken, and saw what a lack of kindness I had toward people at times and how personally He took it. I realized that when I hurt others, I am hurting Him and He will "keep His distance" in terms of the manifestation of His power in my life. Truly, He is the "gentle dove." I have changed!

2. "BECAUSE HE COUNTED ME FAITHFUL."

Paul was thankful because the Lord considered him "trustworthy" (faithful) enough to entrust him with the revelation of the "mystery of Christ" that he was given to bring the Body of Christ to maturity. When God "reveals" truth to us, we should consider ourselves the most blessed people on earth because God's truths cannot be "discovered," they must be "revealed." Paul had experienced the results of the "spirit of wisdom and revelation" in his own life and prayed that the Ephesians would also have the same work of the Spirit in their lives.

> *"Therefore I also, after I heard of your faith in the Lord Jesus and your love for all the saints, do not cease to give thanks for you, making mention of you in my prayers: that the God of our Lord Jesus Christ, the Father of glory, may give to you the spirit of wisdom and revelation in the knowledge of Him, the eyes of your understanding being enlightened; that you may*

> *know what is the hope of His calling, what are the riches of the glory of His inheritance in the saints, and what is the exceeding greatness of His power toward us who believe, according to the working of His mighty power." Ephesians 1:15-19 NKJV*

It is a most humbling thing to think that God is "depending" on someone. When we consider the faithfulness of God, we know beyond doubt that we can "depend" upon Him (Numbers 23:19), that He will not disappoint us when we have placed our lives and situations in His hand. Jesus depended upon the faithfulness of God when He hung on the Cross and said,"Father, into your hands I commit my spirit." He was depending upon the Father to carry Him through the bowels of the earth and after three days, to raise Him up again with a glorified body. It is a humbling thing to think about our children who are utterly dependent upon us a parents when they are babies and small children. But to think that God Almighty is depending upon us to carry out His will in the earth as His "ambassadors," that He would entrust us with the "true riches" of the revelation of His "hidden mysteries" (Colossians 1:25-29), something we could never obtain without His choosing to show us. Paul was deeply thankful for this "trust" by God in the fact that he would not fail to discharge his sacred duty. I imagine as the revelation continued to go "deeper" into the mystery of Christ, and Paul was being overwhelmed by what he was given the privilege to "see into," his gratitude to the Father continued to go deeper as well.

Profound revelation has a "profound" effect upon the sincere hearted person, it makes them eternally thankful.

> *"According to the glorious gospel of the blessed God, which was committed to my trust." 1 Timothy 1:11 NKJV*

3. "PUTTING ME INTO THE MINISTRY."

Paul was thankful because the Father enabled him, and counted him faithful, but also because he was given the opportunity to serve the Body of Christ. One cannot "put themselves into the ministry." The word "ministry" is the Greek word, "diakonia" basically meaning "service." God chooses what type of service we will render in His plans and purposes, and He gifts us accordingly. Romans 11:29

> *"Paul, an apostle of Jesus Christ, by the commandment of God our Savior and the Lord Jesus Christ, our hope," 1 Timothy 1:1 NkJV*

The ministry belongs to the Lord, we are "co workers" together with Him (1 Corinthians 3:6-9). It is the Lord who launches us into ministry and gives us open doors and favor with men. It is the Lord who causes us to become fruitful and prosper in all we lay our hand unto. It is the Lord who gives us an audience to hear our voice and instructs people to be attentive to our words. Over more than three decades of service as an apostle to the Body of Christ, I have seen the futility of those who tried to "put themselves into ministry," those individuals who had a "desire to serve" but were not prepared and proven by the Lord to be trustworthy as of yet. Then there are others with the highest of character, who are in the wrong place at the wrong time trying to enter a ministry not of God's choosing for them. It is sad to see people spend money and put their family thru hardships trying to enter ministry that God has not yet "put them into." When God puts us into ministry, we can have the assurance that we will be heard and have divine favor.

> *"While he yet spake, behold, a bright cloud overshadowed them: and behold a voice out of the cloud, which said, This is my beloved son, in whom I am well pleased; HEAR YE HIM.' Matthew 17:5 KJV*

> *"And Jesus increased in wisdom and stature, and in favor with God and man." Luke 2:52 KJV*

When the Lord Jesus was preparing to go to the Cross, He was giving the disciples final instructions about the coming Holy Spirit in John 14-16, in the middle of the discourse, He assures them of future success and productivity as a result of His putting them into the ministry that He had called, prepared and gifted them to fulfill.

> *"Ye have not chosen me, but I have chosen you, and ordained you, that ye should go and bring forth fruit, and that your fruit should remain: that whatsoever ye shall ask of the Father in my name, he may give it you." John 15:16 NKJV*

Paul was thankful because he had the assurance that comes from "divine placement" in ministry, he could go forward with full confidence that God's blessing would always be manifested and the Kingdom of God would increase. Over the years of ministry in the town God called my family to serve in 1980, we have been thru storms of accusation, betrayal, emotional ups and downs that come from people coming and going in and out of your life. We have had "religious leaders" within the denomination we served at that time try to "put us in the street" when our ministry took a turn that crossed "tradition" with the "truth." We have had times of "being abased" and times of "abundance." We have had rumors spread that effected other area leaders so that they wouldn't offer a hand of fellowship. Like Paul, we were "stoned and taken out of the city to be left for dead." But in all these things, we have survived and thrived by the grace of God, getting people saved, filled, healed and fruitful. All because "God put us into the ministry" and made us "immovable." As we look back on the years of service in our God appointed place of ministry, we are thankful to have been kept by Him who is Faithful and True. The heart of Apostle Paul was a "thankful heart."

Chapter Three

THE SATISFIED HEART

"For I am already being poured out as a drink offering, and the time of my departure is at hand. 7 I have fought the good fight, I have finished the race, I have kept the faith. 8 Finally, there is laid up for me the crown of righteousness, which the Lord, the righteous Judge, will give to me on that Day, and not to me only but also to all who have loved His appearing." 2 Timothy 4:6-8 NKJV

The great apostle is happy as his life is drawing near to its end, because he is "satisfied" that all his work is done and that his life has been spent in pleasing God. What an enticing thought it is to imagine coming to the end of life and being able to rest in our beds with the satisfaction of knowing that God's will had been completed in our lives, releasing the great expectancy of reward that Paul expressed in anticipation of receiving "the crown of righteousness."

Paul understood in totality all that was expected of him by the Lord and used his "check list" to confirm that he had accomplished all. The apostolic grace causes a person to be conscientious regarding the stewardship of the "gifts and calling" bestowed upon them by the Lord. This same conscientiousness can be experienced by all believers who are exposed to apostolic ministry. In many cases, believers can go thru long periods of "wandering in the wildness," not having ascertained what their purpose and calling may be. Paul's list included three areas that sum up his apostolic job description.

1. "I HAVE FOUGHT A GOOD FIGHT."

Paul uses an illustration that was commonly understood for those living under Roman rule and the occupying legions of soldiers. However, he knew that the battle was with a "spiritual army" of demons on earth and spiritual rulers in the heavens. Paul had revelations of the enemies capabilities, strength of forces and the weapons at their disposal against mankind. He knew that his spiritual enemy was a military strategist who made well planned attacks against the Church of Jesus Christ. As an apostle, he was equipped with "super intelligence" from the Holy Spirit that enabled him to "always triumph in Christ" thru the use of the Armor of God, Gifts of the Spirit and Authority of the Believer. Paul was a "spiritual general" who trained his troops to invade enemy territory and "destroy strongholds" with the anointed Word of God, plundering those held captive by the devices of the enemy.

> *"For though we walk in the flesh, we do not war according to the flesh. For the weapons of our warfare are not carnal but mighty in God for pulling down strongholds, casting down imaginations and every high thing that exalts itself against the knowledge of God, bringing every thought into captivity to the obedience of Christ, and being ready to punish all disobedience when your obedience is fulfilled."*
> *2 Corinthians 10:3-6 NKJV*

A "good fight" is the fight that you win. No matter how valiantly you may fight, what matters is who is left standing when the battle is over. Paul was satisfied that he won the battles that he faced in the Name of the Lord in each province of the known world where he established the Church of Christ and left a contingency of disciples to carry on the work of expanding the Kingdom of God in that region. Even though the enemy made many attempts on his life, and he had many scars to prove it, he was victorious and remained alive until "he was ready to be offered up." It is good to be able to "look back" and see that your labor was not in vain, that those you have trained are continuing to bear fruit for the glory of God. That is satisfaction guaranteed.

2. "I HAVE FINISHED THE RACE."

Again Paul uses an illustration from the sports arenas of his day. What he is referring to here is the fact that he was never "disqualified" from the race, but crossed the finish line after staying in his lane for the whole race.

> *"Do you not know that those who run in a race all run, but one receives the prize? Run in such a way that you may obtain it. And everyone who competes for the prize is temperate in all things. Now they do it to obtain a perishable crown, but we for an imperishable crown. Therefore I run thus: not with uncertainty. Thus I fight: not as one who beats the air. But I discipline my body and bring it into subjection, lest, when I have preached to others, I myself should become disqualified." 1 Corinthians 9:24-27 NKJV*

Finishing without disqualifying was an important goal for the apostle, as it should be for all believers as well. The idea of "disqualification" and forfeiting what was promised is then illustrated by the apostle using Israel and their failure to "wholly follow the Lord" in the Wilderness. Paul even lists the reasons for their failure to enter the Promised Land and warns believers not to follow in the footsteps of rebellion and unbelief. I don't believe he is talking to the believers about missing Heaven, but warning them regarding disqualifying from obtaining all the promised blessings God had planned for them in this life. Those blessings may include, "fruitfulness in ministry," "divine health," "financial prosperity" and "protection from the enemy."

> *"Moreover, brethren, I do not want you to be unaware that all our fathers were under the cloud, all passed through the sea, all were baptized into Moses in the cloud and in the sea, all ate the same spiritual food, and all drank the same spiritual drink. For they drank of that spiritual Rock that followed them, and that Rock was Christ. But with most of them God was not well pleased, for their bodies were scattered in the wilderness. Now these things became our examples, to the intent that we should not lust after evil things as they lusted. And do not become idolaters as were some of them. As it is written, "The people sat down to eat and drink, and rose up to play." Nor let us commit sexual immorality, as some of them did, and in one day twenty-three thousand of them fell; not let us tempt Christ, as some of them also tempted, and were destroyed by serpents; nor complain, as some of them also complained, and were destroyed by the destroyer. Now all these things happened to them as examples, and they were written for our admonition, upon whom the ends of the ages have come." 1 Corinthians 10:1-11 NKJV*

The Corinthian believers were in danger of

"disqualification" because of a false sense of security that existed among them, as Paul said,

> *"Therefore, let him who thinks he stands take heed lest he fall." 1 Corinthians 10:12 NKJV*

A number of years ago Leonard Ravenhill, Jr. wrote a book entitled, "Drinking From the River and Dying In the Wilderness." He points out the danger of this false security that comes from enjoying God's blessings in our midst as the Spirit is poured out upon us, while still continuing to indulge in the flesh and sin. The Corinthians were having a great move of God but were not allowing their lifestyle to catch up with all the anointing they were experiencing when together. It is easy to think we must be ok since God is still here blessing us with His Spirit, that God doesn't really mind if we continue living as we did before we were saved. They drank from the river and died in the wilderness." The Israelites had a "river of God" among them that was manifested in five supernatural provisions.

- Supernatural protection of the cloud
- Supernatural deliverance thru the sea
- Supernatural leadership of Moses
- Supernatural food from heaven
- Supernatural water from the Rock

With all of these manifested blessings, they still continued in the five sins that brought disqualification to them, not allowing them to enter the promise land God prepared for them.

- Lusting after evil things
- Idolatry
- Sexual immorality
- Tempting Christ
- Complaining

These sins caused the Israelites to "step out of bounds" and disqualify. When Paul uses the illustration of the "runner" in a race, he is referring to the fact that a runner must remain in his lane, he must stay within boundaries if he is going to finish the race. The lines on either side of the lane are there to make sure the runner has the straightest path to the goal, they are not there to provide a hindrance, but to provide the greatest opportunity to succeed. Often the boundaries set for the believer may seem restrictive, and may cause any rebellion in our hearts to be manifested thru complaining against the way God is dealing with us. However, God knows what we must do in order to obtain all He has planned for us, even when we do not. Boundaries are necessary for training us in self discipline, protocol and submission. Without these things established in our lives, we will not finish our race. Paul was satisfied knowing he had not “crossed the lines” set for him in his journey, but that he had staying within his calling and sphere of ministry, maintaining the example that others could follow for generations to come.

In many competition sports events, there are categories of winners, First Place, Second Place and so on. As a US Marine recruit on Parris Island, SC in 1968, I participated in a “Push Up” competition held between the Platoons in our Company. There were three winners, even though I tried hard for First Place by doing the most pushups, I came in Third Place representing my Platoon. There is a great lesson to be learned in that God has a “First Prize” for all of us to attain in this life. This represents the completion of what we were created for, and put on this planet. It takes a lifetime to obtain First Prize, and if we should disqualify along the way, we may come in with Second or Third Prize at the end of the race. I sincerely believe that we only get “one chance” for First Prize and we must “stay in our lane” the whole way to obtain it. We have all seen those high profile ministers who have fallen into some sin and lost the great momentum that they had in ministry. They may continue in ministry, but it seems that they never get back to the same level of influence and fruit that they were gaining. They are still gifted and anointed, but they have disqualified from the ultimate God had for them, and now they will have to settle for some lesser prize as they continue to serve the Lord. Paul was satisfied that he was a First Prize Winner and had completed his race without disqualification.

3. "I HAVE KEPT THE FAITH."

When we talk about "faith," we usually are referring to the "substance of things hoped for, evidence of things not seen." (Hebrews 11:1) That faith that Jesus was talking about in Mark 11:24, which we commonly call, "The Prayer of Faith."

> *"Therefore I say to you, whatever things you ask when you pray, believe that you receive them, and you will have them." Mark 11:24 NKJV*

Faith in this sense is "believing that you already have what you have not yet seen." This is the faith we use to receive the promises of God. The Amplified Bible says it thus, *"Faith perceives as a real fact that which has not yet been revealed to the five physical senses." Hebrews 11:1 AMP*

Actually, this faith is our Sixth Sense, it is believing with the heart independently of the five physical senses. But Paul was not talking about faith in this sense, he was talking about faith as "the sum total of our beliefs." This is the "faith" Jude was describing in his small letter that was under attack by "heretics and defilers."

> *"Beloved, while I was very diligent to write to you concerning our common salvation, I found it necessary to write to you exhorting you to contend for the faith which was once for all delivered to the saints." Jude 3 NKJV*

Paul was satisfied that "he had kept the faith," he had

helped to preserve the cardinal doctrines of Christianity and establish the believers in "sound doctrine." The word "doctrine" simply means "teaching," Paul had taught them the truth of God without mixture or error and managed to put it in written form for all ages to be blessed by it. Paul's charge to his spiritual son Timothy, was to continue to preach the truth that he had learned from Paul so that the "faith" once delivered to the saints would continue to be delivered to the saints for all time.

> *"I charge you therefore before God and the Lord Jesus Christ, who will judge the living and the dead at His appearing and His kingdom: Preach the Word! Be ready in season and out of season. Convince, rebuke, exhort, with all longsuffering and teaching. For the time will come when they will not endure sound doctrine, but according to their own desires, because they have itching ears, they will heap up for themselves teachers; and they will turn away their ears away from the truth and be turned aside to fables." 2 Timothy 4:1-4 NKJV*

For Paul, "fighting a good fight, finishing the race and keeping the faith" were the three things that brought satisfaction to his aged heart, and prepared him for his departure from this life As apostolic people in today's world, we should use this same "check list" to assure that we will reach the end of our life with the same spiritual satisfaction derived from faithful service to the Lord.

Chapter Four

THE PEACEFUL HEART

"Be anxious for nothing, but in everything by prayer and supplication, with thanksgiving, let your requests be made known to God; and the peace of God which surpasses all understanding, will guard your hearts and minds through Christ Jesus. Finally, brethren, whatever things are true, whatever things are noble, whatever things are just, whatever things are pure, whatever things are lovely, whatever things are of good report, if there is any virtue and if there is anything praiseworthy - meditate on these things. The things which you learned and received and heard and saw in me, these do, and the God of peace will be with you." Philippians 4:6-9 NKJV

Paul had learned three revelations that resulted not only in having the "peace of God" within his heart, but having "the God of peace" with him. No doubt, Paul had practiced these truths thru all the challenges and disappointments he endured in the ministry. As we read about Paul's life, we see that he faced all the adversities that life can throw at a person. He had the physical challenges that resulted from being beaten with rods and lashes, as well as being stoned to death and dragged out of the city where he was left for dead. He faced hunger, the elements, dangerous animals, financial shortage, imprisonment and betrayal by his friends, yet he learned how to live with peace in his heart.

> *"In labors more abundant, in stripes above measure, in prisons more frequently, in deaths often. From the Jews five times I received forty stripes minus one. Three times I was beaten with rods; once I was stoned; three times I was shipwrecked; a night and day I have been in the deep; in journeys often, in perils of waters, in perils of robbers, in perils of my own countrymen, in perils of the Gentiles, in perils in the city, in perils in the wilderness, in perils in the sea, in perils among false brethren; in weariness and toil, in sleeplessness often, in hunger and thirst, in fastings often, in cold and nakedness - besides the other things, what comes upon me daily: my deep concern for all the churches." 2 Corinthians 11:23-28 NKJV*

1. CASTING YOUR CARES UPON THE LORD.

The first truth Paul shares that will result in a peaceful heart, is to "cast your care upon the Lord." When he says to take our worries to God in prayer, he is simply saying, "Tell God about it, and make Him responsible for the outcome." What is it that we usually are anxious about if not the "outcomes" of our situations? Are you worried about losing your job, or if you have already lost it, maybe you are worried about where the next job will come from. Are you anxious about your children's future, or the health of a loved one? The list goes on and on with things that cause people to have mental distress and emotional illnesses. Certainly, Paul had plenty of reasons to get worried since he had already experienced so much pain and anguish in his life, just the thought that some of those things could occur again would be enough to cause anxiety in the strongest person. Yet Paul had learned to let God be responsible for the outcomes of all that could happen in his life.

> *"For this reason I also suffer these things; nevertheless I am not ashamed, for I know whom I have believed and am persuaded that He is able to keep what I have committed to Him until that Day." 2 Timothy 1:12 NKJV*

Rebecca and I (my wife of 40 years) were blessed with four beautiful children, two boys and two girls, Sam, Tim, Beth and Judy. We didn't have any children until after we became born again Christians, so all of our kids were raised in the conservative home of pastors for all of their lives.

They were in church every time the doors opened, the first in and the last to go home. We never played even a "PG" rated movie in our home until our youngest was 16 years old. They all attended and graduated from a Christian School, yet they all left the church when they were old enough to leave home. My wife and I were tempted to quit the ministry because we felt like such failures in the parenting department, after all, how could we teach on "family life" when not one of our children were following in our footsteps to serve Christ. I didn't realize till later in life that putting the ministry before my family left a void in my children for intimacy with me as their father, a void they tried to fill with the "things of the world." Seeing our precious ones in the grip of sin for many years was very hard for us to take, especially knowing that if we had our priorities right in the home, they may have stayed true to their upbringing and avoided so much grief in their own lives. During those early years in ministry, I actually thought I was doing what was best for my family by devoting almost every moment of my time to building the church and helping others with their problems. In spite of all this, God has brought our family back together in Christ and my children are involved in the ministry we have been serving for over 33 years. This happened when Rebecca and I, "let go and let God" take care of it all. We were able to "cast the care" on Him by making Him responsible for the lives of our children. In time, He turned every one of their hearts back to Him, and us. We have the most blessed family one can imagine today, we continually rejoice to sit and listen to them pray with passion and preach with fire. To God be the Glory!

When we make God responsible for the outcome of our situation by telling Him about it and thanking Him for taking care of it for us, in advance, He will do exactly as He promised in His Word to do. Therefore, instead of dreaming of the terrible things that could happen, we are imagining the outcomes to be according to what God promised to do, since He is the One responsible for the situation now.

Paul's second step to a peaceful heart is found in verse 8, which says, "Finally, brethren, whatever things are true, whatever things are noble, whatever things are just, whatever things are pure, whatever things are lovely, whatever things are of good report, if there is any virtue and if there is anything praiseworthy - meditate on these things."

2. CONTROL YOUR THOUGHTS.

Paul knew that Satan would be trying to "devour" us with a mental bombardment of negative thoughts after we have cast our care upon the Lord. This is how the enemy attempts to get us to "take back" the thing we have given to the Lord to take care of for us. Apostle Peter understood this same strategic warfare and explains it to the Christians at Rome in his first letter.

> *"Therefore humble yourselves under the mighty hand of God, that He may exalt you in due time,*

> *casting all your care upon Him, for He cares for you. BE SOBER, BE VIGILANT; because your adversary the devil walks about like a roaring lion seeking whom he may devour. Resist him, steadfast in the faith, knowing that the same sufferings are experienced by your brotherhood in the world." 1 Peter 5:6-8 NKJV*

Again we see the admonition by an apostle to cast our cares, "making God responsible for the outcome," and then, man the watchtower because the enemy will try to devour your thinking with those same anxious thoughts that you have just released to God. However, we can successfully resist the devil by "taking the thoughts captive" and replacing them with the positive thoughts Paul tells us to meditate on in Philippians 4:8, thoughts that issue from contemplation of the Word of God. Someone once said, "*You can't stop a bird from flying over your head, but you can stop it from building a nest in your hair.*" The same is true with our thought life, we can't stop thoughts from coming, but we can stop them from staying. It may take some diligent effort to "resist" the enemy in our thought life, but eventually, he will flee. I remember a time while in Bible College that I was having some severe mental oppression from the enemy. It seemed I couldn't shake the thoughts out of my head that were contrary to the truth of God's Word, and I was losing my peace of mind. The Spirit of God spoke to me and said, "*Break the silence.*" I had been trying to combat the bad thoughts with good thoughts, this was all going on in my head. I never considered opening my mouth and speaking out loud what I wanted my mind to think. I began to verbalize the Word of God and speak out loud to myself the correct thinking, and changed the images running wild in my head. I found out that you cannot "say" one thing and "think" another, when you speak the Word of God you will begin to see it mentally and break the negative thought patterns in your mind that come as a result of meditating on the anxious thoughts placed there by the enemy.

The final step Paul gives for having a peaceful heart is in verse 9, "The things which you learned and received and heard and saw in me, these do, and the God of peace will be with you."

3. COPY YOUR MENTORS.

Paul had proven many truths in his life, he had learned to live by faith in the grace of God to an amazing degree, and had become a model of victory for everyone to follow. He could boldly say, "Follow me as I follow Christ" because the Word of God had become incarnated in him. Notice how detailed his instructions were, things which you learned, things you received, things you heard and things you saw in me "*do these things, and the God of peace will be with you.*" Paul didn't leave out any method of instruction, he covered every possible way that the believers may have gleaned from his life, depending on their relationship with him as an apostle. Some people may have personally interacted with him, others may just have heard people tell about his life, some may have just seen him handling a certain situation, or performing his ministry in some other way. Regardless of the way the truth was communicated, Paul said, "copy it," "do it" and you will have the desired result.

Part of God's plan for raising us to maturity in Christ is to give us "mentors" who can coach us in "Christian living." We are admonished to follow the example of those who have walked with the Lord deeper and longer than we have.

> *"Remember those who rule over you, who have spoken the word of God to you, whose faith follow, considering the outcome of their conduct." Hebrews 13:7 NKJV*

This is a major reason we need to be connected to the larger Body of Christ by faithfully gathering together with a local church, there we will find the "mature models" of the faith that we can observe and safely follow. In so doing we will learn the secrets to living the faith life and walking in the peace of God. In our modern times of technology, the internet has become the source of spiritual training and instruction, but there is no substitute for "relationships" of love and trust such as Jesus had with His disciples, Paul had with Timothy, and Elijah had with Elisha. The Word teaches us this truth in many passages and examples.

> *"He who walks with wise men will be wise, but he companion of fools will be destroyed." Proverbs 13:20 NKJV*

> *"Now when they saw the boldness of Peter and*

> *John, and perceived that they were uneducated and untrained men, they marveled. And they realized that they had been with Jesus." Acts 4:13 NJKV*

In the process of "discipleship," there is no substitute for "observing" another person's life. The relationship is "two way," you observe your mentor, and your mentor observes you. A one way relationship over the internet is not the total answer for coming to maturity in Christ, although it provides good resources for learning.

Paul specifically says that developing the lifestyle of Casting our Cares, Controlling our Thoughts and Copying our Mentors, will cause the "God of peace" to be with us. This brings to mind the story of Noah sending out the dove that returned with an olive branch in its mouth.

> *"He also sent out from himself a dove, to see if the waters had receded from the face of the ground. But the dove found no resting place for the sole of her foot, and she returned into the ark to him, for the waters were on the face of the whole earth. So he put out his hand and took her, and drew her into the ark to himself. And he waited yet another seven days, and again he sent the dove out from the ark. Then the dove came to him in the evening, and behold, a freshly plucked olive leaf was in her mouth; and Noah knew that the waters had receded from the earth." Genesis 8:8-11 NKJV*

There is much symbolism in this passage; the dove represents the Holy Spirit and the olive branch speaks of peace. Noah was limited by what he could see, the waters within range had not receded. But with the help of the Dove, he could know what was beyond his sight, this is what we call "revelation knowledge" and is the ministry of the Holy Spirit to us as believers in Christ. We also see that Noah represents a believer who is "led by the Spirit" and waits for Holy Spirit revelation before making final decisions and actions. Regarding the God of peace, we can learn from this story that God will make His "habitation" where people have learned to trust Him fully by casting their cares, controlling their thoughts and copying their mentors. The Holy Spirit, like a "dove," dwells where there is an atmosphere of faith and trust in God's Word. We find that our communion with God is much more intimate when we have learned to live "worry free" and practice prayer "with thanksgiving." Paul had the God of peace "manifested" in miraculous ways due to his own application of this teaching that he has modeled for all believers.

> *"But be doers of the word, and not hearers only, deceiving yourselves." James 1:22 NKJV*

Chapter Five

THE WARRIOR'S HEART

> *"You therefore must endure hardness as a good soldier of Jesus Christ. No one engaged in warfare entangles himself with the affairs of this life, that he may please him who enlisted as a soldier." 2 Timothy 2:3-4 NKJV*

Paul understood the soldier's life and undoubtedly had all the qualities of a good soldier within himself, including the "warriors" heart, which is a heart willing to fight and die for its beliefs. Paul faced death many times in his defense of the Gospel, as did those who were part of his "apostolic team."

> *"For we do not want you to be ignorant, brethren, of our trouble which came to us in Asia: that we*

> *were burdened beyond measure, above strength, so that we despaired even of life. Yes, we had the sentence of death in ourselves, that we should not trust in ourselves but in God who raises the dead, who delivered us from so great a death, and does deliver us, you also helping together in prayer for us, that thanks may be given by many persons on our behalf for the gift granted to us through many." 2 Corinthians 1:8-11 NKJV*

Paul's understanding of the soldier's life came as a result of living under Roman rule and being a Roman citizen himself. Paul's personal experience with the Roman military included being chained to a soldier during travel, living with a soldier while under house arrest and being saved by two hundred soldiers when the Jew's sought to kill him for speaking the truth of the Gospel. Amazingly, it was Roman soldiers who put him to death after being tried for the same crime. Paul saved a soldier's life by refusing to leave the prison after the angel shook the place apart and loosed him from his stocks, opening the prison door for their escape. By remaining a prisoner after being freed supernaturally, he saved the prison guard who would have been executed for allowing his prisoners to escape. Paul actually saved this soldier twice, once from physical death, and then from spiritual death by leading him to salvation through Christ.

> *"Then he called for a light, ran in, and fell down trembling before Paul and Silas. And he brought them out and said, "Sirs, what must I do to be*

> *saved?" So they said, "Believe on the Lord Jesus Christ, and you will be saved, you and your household." Acts 16:29-30 NKJV*

As a "soldier's soldier," Paul was teaching Timothy the warriors heart as well, who would then impart it to others. The teaching included five areas of warfare that were under attack at that time, and continue to be the target of destruction by the enemy in our day. Much of Paul's writings were actually manuals on spiritual warfare, and showed the way of victory in every battle. Paul was truly a "general" of the faith.

THE BATTLE FOR TRUTH.

Paul has much to say about the believer's relationship with, and responsibility for the truth. There are four things that all believer's must do to win the battle for truth in our day.

- Know the Truth. John 8:30-32; 1 John 2:27
- Love the Truth. 2 Thessalonians 2:8-12
- Defend the Truth. Jude 3; 2 Timothy 2:15
- Speak the Truth. Ephesians 4:15; Acts 4:31

Today, the battle lines are drawn, starting in our educational institutions from Kindergarten to University. Society is being systematically taught to "deny truth" that stems from faith in a Living God as our Creator, to believe in the "man centered" religion of Secular Humanism. This atheistic view is derived from Darwin's hypothesis of "natural selection," and teaches that there are no "absolute truths," especially in regard to "morality." According to these "darkened souls," "truth is relative" and the only truth is what "you believe to be true." Paul makes reference thru the gift of prophecy to the fierce battle for truth being waged by demonic forces in the "latter times" in which we live.

> *"Now the Spirit expressly says that in the latter times some will depart from the faith, giving heed to deceiving spirits and doctrines of demons, speaking lies in hypocrisy, having their own conscience seared with a hot iron, forbidding to marry, and commanding to abstain from foods which God created to be received with thanksgiving by those who believe and know the truth." 1 Timothy 4:1-3 NKJV*

Local churches should major on equipping believers with the truth of God's Word so that they may be competent to wage a good warfare in their daily interaction with people. The Church today must establish believers in "sound doctrine" so that they have a "sharp two edged sword" with which to do battle. Much of current teaching has to do with the "soul realm" because people are so mentally and emotionally distressed due to the "pressure cooker" we call "life." Apostle John told us to minister to the "soul" of people so that they could be "healthy and wealthy," this is good for the individual's happiness.

> *"Beloved, I pray that you may prosper in all things and be in health, just as your soul prospers." 3 John 2 NKJV*

Apostle James also speaks of the need for our "souls to be saved."

> *"Therefore lay aside all filthiness and overflow of wickedness, and receive with meekness the implanted word which is able to save your souls." James 1:21 NKJV*

We need to be healthy both mentally and emotionally, and also to have abundant provisions for our own needs and the needs of others. With this in mind, we need to go beyond just being equipped to live long and pay all our bills on time, but we need to be able to give a defense of the Gospel of Jesus Christ to cult members, agnostics, atheists and everyone else you can think of, as Paul inferred,

> *"I am a debtor both to Greeks and to barbarians, both to wise and to unwise. 15 So, as much as is in me, I am ready to preach the gospel to you who are in Rome also." Romans 1:14-15 NKJV*

We must begin with our children, teaching them Bible doctrine, not just Bible stories. I asked the Lord recently, "Why do we rarely see Muslim children leave their faith, but Christian children seem to stray in droves," the reply I got was, "We teach our children behavior, they teach their beliefs." And it is true, we start them out on behavioral issues and give them the Ten Commandments to memorize. We need to teach them these things for sure, but behavior should stem from beliefs, not the other way around. Our children should understand the Person and Work of Christ, the Person and Work of Holy Spirit, the Authority and Integrity of Scripture by the time they graduate to Youth Group. This would prepare them for the secular humanism they will encounter in High School and College. In order to win the battle for Truth, we must Know it, Love it, Defend it, and Speak it.

THE BATTLE FOR THE FAMILY.

At the time of this writing, twelve states allow same sex marriages as a result of court orders, legislative action or referendums. It seems our society is adrift morally because we have cut the chain connected to the anchor of righteousness, the Holy Bible. If we continue in this moral drift, we will surely shipwreck as civilizations in history have done who follow this same course. Paul taught much about family life, comprised of the union between "one man and one woman" who bring children into this world according to God's order in creation.

> *"For this reason a man shall leave his father and mother and be joined to his wife, and the two shall become one flesh." Ephesians 5:31 NKJV*

It seems that the enemy has been very successful at gaining this foothold among mankind, using one very clear tactic, "eliminate fathers." Many of the mental, physical and social problems that plague us today are directly related to "fatherlessness" according to studies from both Medical doctors and Psychologists. The absence of godly male role models in the home has led to all sorts of violent crime, drug abuse, teen age pregnancy and psychological disorders. Prisons are full of men and women who are bitter towards the father they never knew, or the father who molested and abused them. The battle for the family cannot be won without "fathers" being restored to their place in the family. God spoke about this need to bring a restoration to both the natural and spiritual families of earth thru the Prophet Malachi.

> *"Behold, I will send you Elijah the prophet before the coming of the great and dreadful Day of the Lord. And he will turn the hearts of the fathers to the children, and the hearts of children to the fathers, lest I come and strike the earth with a curse." Malachi 4:5-6 NKJV*

If we are going to win the battle for the family and see healthy, productive children raised up to lead society in the future, men must once again take the God given responsibility to lead their families according to the teaching of Paul the apostle. There are several concise instructions given to men as husbands and fathers, that when applied will bring a great renewal to the biblical idea of "family."

Husbands, love your wives as Christ loved the church. It is interesting that wives don't have to be told to "love their husbands. I believe it is because God gives a man special favor in the eyes of his wife and she loves him from a "gift of love."

> *"He who finds a wife finds a good thing, and obtains favor from the Lord." Proverbs 18:22 NKJV*

I have observed that women will continue to love their man when men consistently don't reciprocate that love. This is the favor of the Lord placed in her heart for that man. But men don't seem to have that gift to love their wives, they must be told to do, and even how to do it.

> *"Husbands, love your wives, just as Christ loved the church and gave himself for her." Ephesians 5:25 NKJV*

It seems that God uses wives as a tool to teach husbands how to love as Christ loves. Men have to "learn to love," while women seem to do it more instinctively. If men learned to love their wives in this way, more women would believe in the biblical model of marriage and want to find that godly man to love them. They would undoubtedly leave the unnatural same sex relationships they look to for some sort of affection and intimacy.

Dwell with your wives according to knowledge. Apostle Peter gave us further insight into successful family life and the relationship between husbands and wives. Peter's revelation corresponds to Paul's when it comes to "how to love your wife."

> *"Husbands, likewise, dwell with them according to understanding, giving honor to the wife, as to the weaker vessel, and as being heirs together of the grace of life, that your prayers may not be hindered." 1 Peter 3:7 NKJV*

It is the responsibility of husbands to "understand" their wives so that they may honor them. Many have taken this scripture to mean that "women are inferior to men" since Peter says they are "weaker." I believe, however, that Peter is talking about "limits," that husbands should understand their wives "limits" and not drive them past the limits of their mental and emotional health. This happens when wives continue to give love to husbands who are not loving them as "Christ loved the church," they are not being "nourished and cherished," they are being made to feel as though they are just a commodity in the man's life to be used whenever he desires. They begin that they are just there to fulfill certain biological and household needs, without honor.

I have observed during my tenure as a pastor, that many women have become depleted mentally and emotionally after years of "giving and not receiving." I like to use the illustration of the "bank." If you keep making withdrawals without making deposits, you will soon be bankrupt. Many women have left their husbands, or given in to some sin or addiction because they have given much more than they received in the relationship, and they simply can't go on for their own sanity. Husbands that love their wives as Christ loved the church, will seek to understand their wife's needs and meet them. They will become proactive by making deposits of tenderness, affirmation and security so that their wives never begin to feel "used." The Church is to be glorious due to how Christ has loved and cared for her, and the wives of Christian men should be as well.

Bring up your children in the nurture and admonition of the Lord. This is a job specifically assigned to the husbands according to this verse in Ephesians.

> *"And you, fathers, do not provoke your children to wrath, but bring them up in the training and admonition of the Lord." Ephesians 6:4 NKJV*

First of all, how do we provoke our children to wrath? It may result from "giving them rules without relationship." Someone has said, "rules without relationship breeds rebellion."Unfortunately, my father didn't learn good parenting skills from his father, so he passed down to his sons some of the negative traits that caused harm to the family. In our home, love was earned thru obedience and was never unconditional. Withholding love and approval was often a tool to control and coerce for the desired behavior. Although the kids may have "cranked out" the right behavior, in their hearts was growing a deep anger and resentment toward their father. When fathers demand obedience instead of winning obedience from their children, the kids grow up without being valued as "human beings" and develop many insecurities and fears. They provoke their children to wrath.

Paul also told the fathers to be involved in "child training" of spiritual things, "nurture and admonition of the Lord" refers to teaching them how to live according to God's principles and have an intimate relationship with the Heavenly Father. Many fathers have delegated this responsibility to the mothers, consequently, many young men view Christianity as a "woman" religion, and they find it hard to believe they can live for God as a man in this world. There is no substitute for what the fathers bring to the well being of their families. If we are going to win the battle for the family, men will have to assume their roles as husbands and fathers, there is no other way.

> *"Behold, children are a heritage from the Lord, the fruit of the womb is a reward. Like arrows in the hand of a warrior, so are the children of one's youth. Happy is the man who has a quiver full of them; they shall not be ashamed, but shall speak with their enemies in the gate." Psalm 127:3-5 NKJV*

The wise Christian father knows that he must prepare his children with a "warriors heart" as well, for one day, they will have to face the enemies of Christ in this world.

THE BATTLE FOR YOUR FAITH.

Paul instructs Timothy to "fight the good fight of faith."

> *"Fight the good fight of faith, lay hold on eternal life, to which you were also called and have*

> *confessed the good confession in the presence of many witnesses." 1 Timothy 6:12 NKJV*

Satan is ever attempting to undermine our faith in the promises and provision of God. This is the faith that "is the substance of things hoped for and the evidence of things not seen." This is the faith that brings healing, miracles, deliverance and provisions to our lives. This is the faith that Jesus compelled people to use, and commended them for using it. This is the faith that is "rewarded" by God with manifestation. F.F. Bosworth said in his healing classic, "Christ The Healer," "God gives a promise, when the promise produces faith, God produces what was promised." The enemy seeks to put our attention on "things that are seen" with the natural eye so that we may not focus on "things which are not seen" those "things" seen by revelation.

> *"While we do not look at the things which are seen, but at the things which are not seen. For the things which are seen are temporary, but the things which are not seen are eternal." 2 Corinthians 4:18 NKJV*

Walking by faith means we walk independently of our five senses and rely totally on God's Word for evidence that we have what we have desired from the Lord. The "prayer of faith" is taught by Jesus in the following verse,

> *"Therefore I say to you, whatever things you ask when you pray, believe that you receive them, and you will have them." Mark 11:24 NKJV*

According to Jesus, we must "believe" we have what we prayed for before we will "see" (with our natural eye) that we have it. The battle for faith is simply this, "to stay in faith" as long as it takes. Satan is working to get us "out of faith" by putting pressure on us to observe the five senses, like Peter when he was walking on the water. He had begun to walk by faith in the word that Jesus spoke to him, "Come," until he began to observe the "wind and rain" which caused fear to enter and he began to sink. This is the enemy's strategy that causes us to lose the "fight of faith" - look at the five senses, fear comes in, and our faith sinks.

Many years ago, John Osteen, the late father of Joel Osteen, tells a story of how he lost a faith battle in his life. He was conducting a leadership conference at his church in Houston, Texas where he expected hundreds of pastor to attend. He prayed and asked God for two cows to butcher and prepare for the pastors. After a week or two when the cows had not yet "appeared," he told his secretary to purchase the two cows. That night, in a dream, Pastor Osteen saw two large snakes, each had the outline of a cow in it. The Lord spoke to him and said, "You let the devil steal your cows." He had started out in faith, "believing he had two cows he had prayed for," but he got impatient and let go of the answer, he didn't "stay in faith long enough." Winning the battle for faith means we must be able to look past the five senses and see with the eye of faith (our sixth sense) and continue to believe we "have" what we asked for, until it is manifested in the natural realm. Nothing else is "faith."

THE BATTLE FOR YOUR SOUL.

The apostle informs the believers at Rome regarding the warfare against their soul, that when won, will bring great glory to God.

> *"Beloved, I beg you as sojourners and pilgrims, abstain from fleshly lusts which wage war against the soul, having your conduct honorable among the Gentiles, that when they speak against you as evildoers, they may, by your good works which they observe, glorify God in the day of visitation." 1 Peter 2:11-12 NKJV*

The soul is comprised of mind, will and emotions. Another way to say it would be, "thoughts, feelings, and choices." So how does the devil work his will upon our souls and cause us to lose our testimony before the world that would otherwise be the thing that convinces them to believe in God for themselves. First we must recognize what the devil is using against us, the "fleshly lusts" that already exist in our carnal nature. It is only the spirit man that has been affected in the New Birth, being made a totally new creation. The "outward man" our human bodies, have developed desires based upon the former life of sin, and it will continue to desire these things all thru this life until we receive our glorified bodies in the resurrection at the return of Jesus Christ.

> *"For our citizenship is in heaven, from which we also eagerly wait for the Savior, the Lord*

> *Jesus Christ, who will transform our lowly body that it may be conformed to His glorious body, according to the working by which He is able even to subdue all things to Himself." Philippians 3:20-21 NKJV*

The warfare goes like this, if we allow the desires of our flesh to constantly be "on our minds," those ungodly thoughts will soon produce "feelings" that lead to "actions." So the process of losing the battle for the soul is "thoughts, feelings and actions," in that order. For example, if we are trying to lose weight and our mind is continually thinking of a huge slice of chocolate cake, we will soon have an irresistible craving aroused that will lead to the Bakery. If immoral thoughts continually come to mind and we dwell on them, unholy passion will fan into flame and we will be too weak to resist if the "wrong" opportunity presents itself.

The battle of the soul against fleshly lusts is won by "taking thoughts captive immediately" before they "light a fire" in us. We have the power to control our thought life and to resist temptation.

> *"But each one is tempted when he is drawn away by his own desires and enticed. Then, when desire has conceived, it gives birth to sin, and sin, when it is full grown, brings forth death." James 1:14 NKJV*

The world is waiting to accuse us as believers, as Peter

told the Romans who were being spoken of as "evildoers." This is parallel to our situation today as the "liberal" controlled media make Christians out to be the "evildoers" in our society, even labeling us as potential terrorists. The goal of this brainwashing is to have an excuse to eliminate us from existence, just like the enemy wants to eliminate the Jewish state from the face of the earth, he desires the same for Christians. By losing the battle for the soul, we are helping the enemy to find cause to condemn us, we must win this battle and live the Christ life that is within at all times, letting the light of our new life in Christ shine. When our soul is controlled by fleshly desire, it is like putting a "lampshade" over the light of God's life in our spirit.

THE BATTLE FOR YOUR MINISTRY.

This is the last area that we will share where a battle is raging against the believer. Satan would love to steal away our ministry so that we may not be fruitful servants who bring glory to God thru the advancement of His Kingdom. Paul is speaking to his spiritual son, Timothy, and admonishing him to beware of the "schemes of the devil" that worked effectively in the lives of others whom God had called to service in leadership.

> *"This charge I commit to you, son Timothy, according to the prophecies previously made concerning you, that by them you may wage a good warfare, having faith and a good conscience, which some having rejected, concerning the faith have suffered shipwreck, of*

whom are Hymenaeus and Alexander, whom I delivered to Satan that they may learn not to blaspheme." 1 Timothy 1:18-20 NKJV

As an "apostle," Paul is both a "spiritual father," teaching others how to reproduce sons and daughters, and, a "spiritual general" teaching his sons and daughters about warfare. Apparently, the two men mentioned were also "spiritual sons" of Paul who had fallen prey to "seducing spirits" and were rejecting the true faith. As a spiritual authority in their lives, Paul was authorized to "excommunicate" them from the covering of the Church, exposing them to Satan who would soon try to destroy them. All this was in hopes that they would come to their senses, repenting and being restored.

Paul uses them as an example to Timothy, making him very aware that Satan would also like to "take him out" as well. He gives him the proper instructions that will safeguard his son from "shipwreck" by, continuing to acknowledge his relationship to Paul as his spiritual father, and by continuing to believe the prophetic words that were spoken over him at the time of his release into ministry. These truths are paramount in our spiritual battles, because our relationship to spiritual covering provides protection from deception of the enemy. Spiritual discernment remains sharp while we stay in proper alignment to the authority of godly leadership in our lives. Also, the prophetic word from God releases the power of God into your life and begins to form your destiny.

> *"For though you may have ten thousand instructors in Christ, yet you do not have many fathers: for in Christ Jesus I have begotten you through the gospel. Therefore, I urge you, imitate me." 1 Corinthians 4:15-16 NKJV*

> *"Do not neglect the gift that is in you, which was given to you by prophecy with the laying on of hands of the eldership." 1 Timothy 4:14 NKJV*

> *"So shall My word be that goes forth out of My mouth; it shall not return to Me void, but it shall accomplish what I please, and it shall prosper in the thing for which I sent it." Isaiah 55:11 NKJV*

Paul affirms his own victory, and the victory in warfare that is available to all believers in Christ who follow the wisdom of apostolic teaching.

> *"Now thanks be to God who always leads us in triumph in Christ, and through us diffuses the fragrance of His knowledge in every place." 2 Corinthians 2:14 NKJV*

Chapter Six

THE GENEROUS HEART

The early apostles had a revelation of the "Generosity of God." When Paul was speaking to the elders of the Ephesians church, he explained the value he placed upon "giving."

> *"I have coveted no one's silver or gold or apparel. Yes, you yourselves know that these hands have provided for my necessities, and for those who were with me. I have shown you in every way, but laboring like this, that you must support the weak. And remember the words of the Lord Jesus, that He said, "It is more blessed to give than to receive." Acts 20:33-35 NKJV*

Why in Paul's view, was it more "blessed" to give

than to receive? I believe we can sum it up by saying that when we receive, we "get" something, but when we give we "become" something. What we "become" is infinitely more valuable than what we "get" in this life. Our goal is to become more like God in our attitudes and actions, and by becoming a generous person, we are becoming more like Him who is the greatest and most generous giver of all.

> *"For God so loved the world that He GAVE His only begotten Son, that whoever believes in Him should not perish but have everlasting life." John 3:16 NKJV*

It would have been great enough if God had just given us His Son to redeem us from our sins so we could escape Hell and be with Him in Heaven, but after giving us Jesus, he freely gave us "all things."

> *"He who did not spare His own Son, but delivered Him up for us all, how shall he not with Him also freely give us all things?" Romans 8:32 NKJV*

Paul told the Ephesians that God was not just "merciful," but that He was "rich in mercy." He explains the extravagant giving heart of God, who after forgiving us our sins, "raised us up to share the Throne of His Exalted Son." This would be like you and I appearing before a judge for a crime we were convicted of, and being totally forgiven and freed from the penalty. That would be merciful, and something to shout about, but what if the judge followed up by saying, "Now that you are forgiven, we are going to make you the

Mayor of the City." That would be a generous move toward us, and much more than we ever expected or deserved. This is what Father God has done for us, after forgiving us, He positioned us to experience the "riches of His kindness toward us in the ages to come." "What generosity is this?"

> *"But God, who is rich in mercy, because of His great love with which He loved us, even when we were dead in trespasses, made us alive together with Christ (by grace you have been saved) and raised us up together, and made us sit together in the heavenly places in Christ Jesus, that in the ages to come He might show the exceeding riches of his grace in His kindness toward us in Christ Jesus." Ephesians 2:4-7 NKJV*

We have no "earthly" idea how good it is going to get in the future with God, but I think it is safe to say that we are going to be extremely happy and content forever because of His good plans for us.

Paul knew that "generosity" was a key to the revival going on in the early church, the reason being, *God shows up the strongest where the people are most like Him.* Think about it, where are you the most comfortable, among strangers, or people you can relate too? We read in the Book of Acts how these people who were freshly impacted by the Life of God, and filled with the Holy Spirit were so "spontaneously" generous. They went way beyond just giving what they "didn't need anyway," to selling their own property and giving it to the other believers who were in need of the basic essentials of life. For this reason, there was "great grace" released in their midst and the miraculous continued to manifest. Notice in the following passages how a verse on "power" is sandwiched between two verses on "generous giving."

> *"And the multitude of them that believed were of one heart and of one soul: neither said any of them that ought of the things which he possessed was his own; but they had all things in common." And with great power gave the apostles witness of the resurrection of the Lord Jesus: and great grace was upon them all. Neither was there any among them that lacked: for as many as had possessions of lands or houses sold them, and brought the prices of the things that were sold, and laid them down at the apostles' feet: and distribution was made unto every man according as he had need." Acts 4:32-35 NKJV*

It seems that generosity was a significant theme in the minds of the apostles, and that they role modeled this virtue as the standard for the believers to follow, always looking for opportunity to commend openly those who's practice it was to be generous. The Macedonian Christians were prime examples of people who wouldn't be refused the opportunity to give, even out of their own deep poverty, they gave generously to help the suffering "family of God" in Jerusalem. Paul was deeply moved by their "godliness" in this regard and provided the means for their offering to taken to relieve their brothers and sisters in Christ. This great generosity was a manifestation of the "grace of God" operating in them.

Jesus commented on the generosity of a certain widow's giving as He stood near the Temple treasury observing the giving practices of people.

> *"Now Jesus sat opposite the treasury and saw how the people put money into the treasury. And many who were rich put in much. Then one poor widow quadrans. So He called His disciples to Himself and said to them, "Assuredly, I say to you that this poor widow has put in more than all those who have given to the treasury: for they all put in out of their abundance, but she out of her poverty put in all that she had, her whole livelihood." Mark 12:41-44 NKJV*

Jesus also valued the quality of "generosity" in the lives of people during His time on earth. He defines generosity by the amount given in relation to the amount possessed. Rich people may give large amounts to charities, some for the right reasons, and others for the tax benefits they receive from the Government. God always looks at the motives behind our actions and rewards us accordingly. For this poor widow to give all she had, meant that she placed others needs above her own, she was free from the spirit of poverty, she had great faith in God to provide for her own needs.

These are the characteristics of someone with a "generous heart." These individuals are always looking for ways to give more than is expected or even needed. We have seen the spirit of generosity in people who didn't have much money to give, but they gave of themselves time and again with acts of service, fulfilling their own responsibilities and then doing the work that others left undone as well. This is generosity. When people are looking for ways to "withhold more than is due," it is the "spirit of poverty" at work in their lives.

> *"There is one who scatters, yet increases more: And there is one who withholds more than is right, but it leads to poverty. The generous soul will be made rich, and he who waters will also be watered himself." Proverbs 11:25-26 NKJV*

Paul commended the Philippians for their generosity in support of his ministry when they gave beyond what was expected, and filled up what was lacking in Paul's needs due to the lack of giving on the part of other Macedonians. Paul gave a great prophetic word to the Philippians that was triggered by their generous giving.

> *"But I rejoiced in the Lord greatly that now at last your care for me has flourished again; though you surely did care, but you lacked opportunity. Not that I speak in regard to need, for I have learned in whatever state I am, to be content: I know how to be abased, and I know how to abound. Everywhere and in all things I*

> *have learned both to be full and to be hungry, both to abound and to suffer need. I can do all things through Christ who strengthens me. Nevertheless you have done well that you shared in my distress. Now you Philippians know also that in the beginning of the gospel, when I departed from Macedonia, no church shared with me concerning giving and receiving but you only. For even in Thessalonica you sent aid once and again for my necessities. Not that I seek a gift, but I seek the fruit that abounds to your account. Indeed I have all and abound. I am full, having received from Epaphroditus the things sent from you, a sweet smelling aroma, an acceptable sacrifice, well pleasing to God. And my God shall supply all your need according to His riches in glory by Christ Jesus." Philippians 4:10-19 NKJV*

Generosity is the result of the "love of God being shed abroad in our hearts by the Holy Spirit" (Romans 5:5). Paul expressed his deep love for the Christians at Corinth, the love of a "father" for his children which will withhold nothing in terms of the love they needed, and the form in which it would be manifested.

> *"Now for the third time I am ready to come to you. And I will not be burdensome to you; for I do not seek yours, but you. For the children ought not to lay up for the parents, but the parents for the children. And I will very gladly*

> *spend and be spent for your souls; though the more abundantly I love you, the less I am loved."*
> *2 Corinthians 12:14-15 NKJV*

This is a love that keeps on giving until there is "nothing left to give." This is the Generous Heart of an Apostle, a life completely poured out for Christ's Body.

Chapter Seven

THE PERSUADED HEART

Paul has become persuaded of his beliefs both by "authority" and "experience," as he relates to us in this powerful passage in Romans where the apostle reveals three areas in which he is fully persuaded about his relationship to God. As an apostle, he was fully convinced of the truth he lived and preached so that those he ministered to would be delivered from unbelief and enter into a full faith in God.

> *"What then shall we say to these things? If God is for us, who can be against us? He who did not spare His own Son, but delivered Him up for us all, how shall He not with Him also freely give us all things? Who shall bring a charge against God's elect? It is God who justifies. Who is he who condemns? It is Christ*

> *who died, and furthermore is also risen, who is even at the right hand of God, who also makes intercession for us. Who shall separate us from the love of Christ? Shall tribulation, or distress, or persecution, or famine, or nakedness, or peril, or sword? As it is written: "For Your sake we are killed all day long; We are counted as sheep for the slaughter." Yet in all these things we are more than conquerors through Him who loved us. For I am persuaded that neither death nor life, nor angels nor principalities nor powers, nor things present nor things to come, nor height nor depth, nor any other created thing, shall be able to separate us from the love of God which is in Christ Jesus our Lord." Romans 8:31-39 NKJV*

The Greek word for "*persuaded*" actually means to be "*convinced by authority and experience*." Paul is saying that his "persuasion" has come as a result of his acceptance of the "authority of God's revelation in Christ," which has become the "Word of God" to him. And, from his experience as a person of faith who has learned to apply the Word to his life daily and experience the freedom that comes from "walking in truth." Apostle John also affirmed the necessity of "experiencing the truth" in his last letter,

> *"I have no greater joy than to hear that my children walk in truth." 3 John 4 NKJV*

The fully persuaded heart is formed in us as a result of understanding the "authority of God's Word," and "walking in the truth" of the Word for ourselves. There is no substitution for the "application" of the truth to our lives, as James said regarding those who only "hear, but do not apply" the Word to life.

> *"But be doers of the word, and not hearers only, deceiving yourselves." James 1:22 NKJV*

It appears that all three of these apostles, Paul, John and James were giving the same message to the saints under their care, "*it is necessary to act on God's Word in order to experience the full benefits of the Word.*" Christians may assent to their belief in the "authority of scripture" as the infallible Word of God, but it will not produce the results of the finished work of Christ until acted upon. The writer of Hebrews describes the reason that a whole generation "died in the wilderness," never having entered God's best for their lives even though it was already provided by the loving Heavenly Father. It was due to "unbelief" in their hearts. The word actually means "unpersuadable," they could not be persuaded to act on God's Word, but instead only assented to "hearing God's voice." They knew it was God who was speaking, but refused to act in faith upon what was spoken, expecting God to perform what He had spoken to them.

> *"Let us therefore fear, lest, a promise being left us of entering into his rest, any of you should seem to come short of it. For unto us was the gospel preached, as well as unto them: but the word preached did not profit them, not being mixed*

> *with faith in them that heard it." Hebrews 4:1-2 NKJV*

Paul had been a "doer of the word," he had "mixed faith" with what he heard, and as a result he experienced the victory in Christ and was "fully persuaded" of the following three truths from our text in Romans. The person who has "walked in truth" and experienced the results of the integrity of God's Word, will be a fully persuaded person.

THERE IS NO SHAME IN CHRIST

> *"Who shall lay anything to the charge of God's elect? It is God that justifies. Who is he that condemneth? It is Christ that died, yea rather, that is risen again who is even at the right hand of God, who also maketh intercession for us." Romans 8:33-34 NKJV*

Paul is fully persuaded of his standing in grace before the Throne of God. He knows that God is the Judge, and that He has justified believers who have accepted the finished work of Christ in His substitutionary work on the cross. Paul will accept no condemnation, no shame in the Presence of God, either from past sins, or present shortcomings. Shame for what we have done as sinners, and sometimes shame for what others have done to us where there have been violations of our dignity as human beings, have all been "removed" from our conscience by the Blood of Christ. Paul is fully persuaded of his "acceptance in the beloved" and had learned how to live "shamelessly" in the Presence of God. When a believer understands this revelation, they are immediately set free from a "performance based" relationship with God, and can "enter into the rest" of our "position in Christ." No amount of "good works" can ever remove "shame" from our conscience, it is only the Blood of Christ that assures us of perfect forgiveness and acceptance by the Father. Paul was persuaded that he would never be "condemned" again while remaining in Christ by faith. He had no sense of inferiority when approaching God, but came with "boldness to the throne of grace" knowing that he was on equal standing with Jesus Christ who had "prepared a place for him" in the Presence of God. Paul had learned to live in his position as a "son of God."

Being "In Christ," means that we share the same "position" with the Father as Jesus, Himself. Can Christ be "ashamed," feel "inferior" or be "condemned"? Of course not, He lived a "sinless life" and had nothing to be ashamed of, or condemned for. When we have accepted Him, we have accepted the same position with God as His. We can be as free from shame, inferiority and condemnation as He is, because our acceptance is not based upon how we lived our lives, but upon how He lived His.

> *"In my Father's house are many mansions: if it were not so, I would have told you. I go to prepare a place for you. And if I go and prepare a place for you, I will come again, and receive you unto myself: that where I am, there ye may be also." John 14:2-3 NKJV*

THERE IS NO SHORTAGE IN CHRIST

"He that spared not his own Son, but delivered him up for us all, how shall he not with him also freely give us all things." Romans 8:32 NKJV

In Paul's thinking, if God would not even spare His Son in order to meet the need we had as lost sinners, what would He withhold from us in order to live fruitful lives here on earth. Paul was persuaded that God will "freely give us all things," that He was just as ready to give us anything that "pertains to life and godliness," as He was ready to send His Son to the cross for us. This is an amazing truth, something that needs to be understood by many of God's children in the church today. Many still think that God only cares about getting them to heaven when they die, but the rest of life here on earth is something we will have to deal with on our own and "make the best of it." However, the word teaches us that salvation included meeting all of our needs in spirit, soul and body. This means that there is no shortage of healing, prosperity, deliverance, joy, peace and total victory. All these things have been as abundantly provided by God as has the forgiveness of our sins. The only real problem we have is revealed by the Prophet Hosea.

"My people are destroyed by a lack of knowledge." Hosea 4:6 NKJV

People that still have a shortage mentality due to a lack of knowledge about God and His plans for us, remind me of a story I heard years ago about a man traveling by boat to the US from Europe.

"A certain man decided to travel to America, after he purchased his ticket on the boat, he only had enough money left to purchase some cheese and crackers on the voyage. Each day he would walk past the Dining Room and look in to see what people were having as they sat down to sumptuous meals for Breakfast, Lunch and Dinner. Knowing he had no money left, he would walk on deck eating his cheese and crackers, all the while letting God know that he was not ungrateful even though he only had such meager fare during the journey. When they landed and were leaving the ship, the Captain asked the gentleman if he didn't like the food on board since he had noticed the man never eating in the Dining Room. The man said, "Oh no, Captain. You see, I only had enough money for cheese and crackers after purchasing my ticket." The Captain replied, "I am sorry that you never read the back of your ticket to find out that all your meals were included in the price."

Our redemption through the Blood of Christ has paid the price for every need we may have now and in eternity. That is why Paul said God would freely give us all things, it was because Christ had already paid for it all. We must realize that God never thinks in terms of shortage. When He created this earth as a habitation for man, He put within it all the resources we would need for as long as He intends us to be here. It is only mismanagement, greed and wastefulness that create shortage in this world. When Jesus performed miracles of provision, He always provided an abundance, not just "barely enough." If it was "loaves and fishes," there were basketfuls left over, and if it was a "catch of fish," there were so many that the boats were sinking. Paul had a revelation of abundance when he wrote to the Corinthians with instructions about giving and receiving.

> *"And God is able to make all grace abound toward you: that ye, always having all sufficiency in all things, may abound to every good work:" 2 Corinthians 9:8 NKJV*

Paul emphasized that "sufficiency" included "abundance in all things." He was persuaded that there was no shortage in the plan of God for His people, even though he at times experienced lack while he was waiting on the provision to come forth. Paul lived with a revelation of a "full supply" at all times, he walked by faith and not by sight, always resulting in his provisions being manifested whether by his hand, or the hands of others.

THERE IS NO SEPARATION IN CHRIST

Paul now concludes his thoughts in this passage by sharing that he is fully persuaded about God's undying love for him and all believers. Christians in the First Century experienced many hardships as the new message of Christianity was taking the world by storm, upsetting all the existing systems including many of the social issues of the day where values were derived from pagan beliefs.

Those who were challenged by the new emphasis brought by the message of the Kingdom of God, often retaliated violently, inflicting great harm on God's people. Paul himself, had been beaten, stoned, shipwrecked, left naked, hungry and imprisoned for his faith. In all these things, he never doubted the love God had for him. It is Satan who will fill our minds with accusatory thoughts toward God in times of persecution in our lives, telling us that God must not really care about us or He would not permit such suffering. The truth is, when we suffer, God suffers with us because of His great love for us. When the forces of light and darkness collide in this world, just like in any war, there will be pain and suffering that is unavoidable. God's love for us cannot be measured only by our experiences in life, because there are times when we all "feel" forsaken or abandoned due to the current trial we are facing. Instead, God has revealed Himself to us thru Christ. When we see Jesus in the four gospels, we see God in action, reaching out to people who are hurting, restoring lives and giving hope. God is love, and there can never be any other attitude towards us but "love."

> *"Beloved, let us love one another, for love is of God: and everyone who loves is born of God and knows God. He who does not love does not know God, for God is love." 1 John 4:7-8 NKJV*

We may be separated at the moment from our health, loved ones, resources or expected position in life, but we are never separated from His love. That is what keeps us moving in faith while we deal with the challenges of life, "God loves me, and He will provide a way of escape for me. He will enable me to bear up under anything, in a "fiery furnace," He still loves me. In a "lion's den," He still loves me. As a "slave in Potiphar's house," He still loves me. Paul list's the things he had gone through which were not able to separate him from God's love.

> *"Shall tribulation, or distress, or persecution, or famine, or nakedness, or peril, or sword? Nay, in all these things we are more than conquerors through him that loved us. For I am persuaded, that neither death, nor life, nor angels, nor principalities, nor powers, nor things present, nor things to come, nor height, nor depth, nor any other creature, shall be able to separate us from the love of God, which is in Christ Jesus our Lord." Romans 8:35, 37-39 NKJV*

Paul was persuaded by "authority and experience," he knew there was No Shame, No Shortage and No Separation. He could impart these apostolic truths that he had worked out in his life experience, and as a result, he could raise up people who would also be able to "stand in the evil day."

Chapter Eight

THE FATHER'S HEART

The New Testament reveals three relationships with "fathers" in our lives.

- The Heavenly Father
- The earthly father
- The spiritual father

As a "spiritual father," Paul often referred to his relationship with those he considered to be his "sons" in the faith, and his "spiritual children." In Paul's letters to the Corinthians, he reminds them that he is their "spiritual father" because he had brought them to faith in Christ.

"I do not write these things to shame you, but as

my beloved children I warn you. For though you might have ten thousand instructors in Christ, yet you do not have many fathers; for in Christ Jesus I have begotten you through the gospel. Therefore I urge you, imitate me." 1 Corinthians 4:14-16 NKJV

Being a father is a most responsible position in both the natural and spiritual realms. In the natural world, when we are responsible for the birth of a child, we assume that the person will also be responsible for raising the child, including caring for all of its needs until adulthood. In today's society, the number one cause of our societal problems, is the absence of "fathers" who are responsible for their children. This simply means that men may have the biological capability to sire children, but not have a "father's heart" to care for them after birth. The welfare roles are burdened with fatherless children who must be cared for by the State, and the prisons are full of young men and women who cannot tell of a healthy relationship with their earthly father.

The same can be true in the Church of Jesus Christ today, when we have gifted ministers who can birth people into the Kingdom of God, but who don't have the parenting skills to raise them to spiritual adulthood. A true spiritual father will be faithful to raise their spiritual children to maturity in Christ and provide the love, nurture, admonishment and exhortation that all children need when growing up. Paul gives the qualities of good spiritual fathering in his letter to the Thessalonians.

> *"You are witnesses, and God also, how devoutly and justly and blamelessly we behaved ourselves among you who believe; as you know how we exhorted, and comforted and charged every one of you, as a father does his own children." 1 Thessalonians 2:10-11 NKJV*

As a spiritual father, Paul was concerned that he had given them a godly example to follow as we see in verse 10, but also that he had carried out the functions of fathering to exhort, comfort and charge them in the things of God in verse 11. Paul was a very responsible spiritual father who had "maturity" in mind for his "sons and daughters."

So how does a ''father's heart" form in an individual? Paul gives the answer in his letter to the Philippians when talking about his spiritual son, Timothy, who was the best example of "sonship" that Paul could set before others.

> *"But I trust in the Lord Jesus to send Timotheus shortly unto you, that I also may be of good comfort, when I know you state. For I have no man likeminded, who will naturally care for you state. For all seek their own, not the things which are Jesus Christ's. But ye know the proof of him, that, as a son with the father, he hath served with me in the gospel." Philippians 2:19-22 NKJV*

Of all Paul's protégés, he could only find one who had developed the "father's heart" and would provide the same care for the Philippians that he would have given, had he been able to see them personally. How did Timothy obtain the same heart that was in Paul? It was by becoming a "spiritual son." The only way to get the "heart of a father" is by becoming a "son" in relationship. Timothy had become Paul's "son in the faith" when he adopted him from his mother's household, and then raised him up spiritually to "know his ways in Christ."

> *"For this reason I have sent Timothy to you, who is my beloved and faithful son in the Lord, who will remind you of my ways in Christ, as I teach everywhere in every church." 1 Corinthians 4:17 NKJV*

When the heart of a father is formed in the son, the son will not only follow the ways of his father, but will also do things with the same motives as his father. He has become "like his father" in spirit and truth.

When Jesus said that the "Father seeketh such that worship Him, in spirit and in truth," I believe this is what he was talking about. A true son of God that has grown up in relationship with his father, will not only reflect the ways, representing the "truth," but he will also manifest the character of the father, representing the "spirit." In other words, the son not only "knows" (truth) that the father knows, but he has "become" (spirit) what the father is. As a son Himself, Jesus had become like his Father in "spirit and in truth," and could say, "if you have seen Me, you have seen the Father." A true son will "re-present" the father that raised him up and sent him out.

Even Jesus went through the process of growth to maturity to become a "spiritual father" as well. The Prophet Isaiah tells us that Jesus followed the same path to maturity that all God's sons must follow.

> *"For unto us a child is born, unto us a son is given: and the government shall be upon his shoulder; and his name shall be called Wonderful, Counselor, The mighty God, The everlasting Father, The Prince of Peace." Isaiah 9:6 NKJV*

Jesus was a "child" who became a "son," who became a "father."

Of course, He wasn't a natural father, since he was never married. But he became a spiritual father to His disciples whom he called, and raised up to stand in His place when He left for heaven to become our High Priest. In Jesus' prayer found in John 17, we find Him praying for the sons he had raised, who were now ready to carry on their responsibilities under the leadership of the Holy Spirit.

> *"I have manifested thy name unto the men which thou gavest me out of the world; thine they were, and thou gavest them me: and they have kept thy word. Now they have known that*

> *all things whatsoever thou hast given me are of thee." John 17:6-7 NKJV*

Jesus had learned the "heart of the father" by being in an intimate relationship with Him, and serving the Father's will and vision.

> *"No man has seen God at any time: the only begotten Son, which is in the bosom of the Father, he hath declared him." John 1:18 NKJV*

Jesus could reveal what the Father was like because of his relationship to Him as a Son. He had become like His Father in "spirit and truth." That is why He could explain to his disciples what the Father expected from "worship," it was a lifestyle that represented the Father's "Person and Principles."

Timothy had learned the same things from being in relationship with Paul, and "serving" as part of Paul's ministry team. Paul said, "*As a son with the father, he has served with me in the gospel.*"

We see this principle working in Elijah and Elisha, the classic Old Testament example of spiritual fathers and sons. When Elijah was about to be taken up to heaven in a whirlwind, Elisha asked to become a "spiritual son" to Elijah and not just a servant in his ministry. When Elisha asked for a "double portion" of the spirit, he was actually asking him how to become a "spiritual son." We know this because of scripture that tells us the "double portion" is an inheritance for a son.

> *"But he shall acknowledge the son of the hated for the firstborn, by giving him a double portion of that he hath: for he is the beginning of his strength: the right of the firstborn is his." Deuteronomy 21:17 NKJV*

Elisha knew that the double portion could only be given to a son, so he was really asking to become a son of Elijah. He knew that becoming a son involved not only "obtaining'" what his spiritual father had in terms of anointing, but it also meant "becoming" what he was in terms of his heart. Elisha would need to have the same pure heart and motives that Elijah had while serving God. He had to be "proven," just like Timothy was with Paul. The "son" must learn to love the people like the "father" loves them. There can be no self seeking agendas that motivate ministry, this is why Paul selected Timothy to represent him to the Philippians.

> *"For I have no man like minded, who will naturally care for your state. For all seek their own, not the things which are Jesus Christ's." Philippians 2:20-21 NKJV*

The "father's heart" is not self seeking, it will always do what is in the best interest of others. Father's do not use their children to "make their lives better," or "to make their dream come to pass." Fathers live for the welfare and promotion of their children, they serve the destiny of their children. This is the true meaning of a 'well worn' verse so often quoted in parenting classes.

> *"Train up a child in the way he should go: and when he is old, he will not depart from it." Proverbs 22:6 NKJV*

Just like a biological parent should recognize what talents their children have been given, and direct them to develop those qualities, a spiritual parent should discern what "gifts and callings" God has deposited within the sons and daughters entrusted to them, so that they may resource them for full use of the anointing in their lives. When a leader has not developed a "father's heart" in ministry, they will seek to use the people God has given them to build their own destiny. They will value people only as long as they are an "asset" to the ministry. But when someone is not contributing to the "vision," that person is often considered unworthy of their best efforts to better their lives. God the Father pours out His blessings upon the "just and unjust" alike, because He loves everyone equally. When a leader has the "father's heart," they will do likewise.

An apostle with a "father's heart" will build "family," not just an organization or ministry. Apostle Paul understood and taught that the Church was:

- The Body of Christ
- An Army

- A Temple of God
- The Bride of Christ
- The Pillar and Ground of Truth
- A Chaste Virgin
- A Royal Priesthood
- A Holy Nation

But, above all, the Church is the "Family of God," the Church of the Firstborn.

> *"For this cause I bow my knees unto the Father of our Lord Jesus Christ, of whom the whole family in heaven and earth is named." Ephesians 3:14-15 NKJV*

All the metaphors of the Church will play out in time, but "*family is forever.*" The reason for creation was the "Father Heart of God," He wanted a family to lavish His love upon, thru Jesus Christ the "firstborn of many brethren," He has obtained the family He desired. In this passage, Paul was praying for the "family of God" to comprehend the extent of Father's love for them so that they might be filled with all the "fullness of God." This would result in the Family being able to love to the same extent that they had been loved by the Father. This was the desire of Jesus when He prayed His final prayer in preparation for the crucifixion, that his followers would know to what extent they were loved by the Father.

> *"I in them, and thou in me, that they may be made perfect in one: that the world may know that thou hast sent me, and hast loved them, as thou hast loved me." John 17:23 NKJV*

Apostles with a "father's heart" will role model, teach and impart the Father's love to His Family.

ABOUT THE AUTHOR

John Polis was saved and filled with Holy Spirit in 1974 during the Jesus Movement. He attended Dayton Bible College and graduated with a B.A. in Biblical Studies in 1980, after which he became pastor of a Pentecostal church in West Virginia.

In 1983, John had an encounter that transitioned him into the ministry of Apostle. Afterwards, he began to travel as an Evangelist and International Bible Teacher.

Among the works established was Eldoret Bible College in Kenya, Africa, which was birthed in 1998 and has graduated over 2500 students with undergraduate and graduate degrees. Students have planted more than 600 churches throughout Africa to date, some of which have more than 5000 in attendance. John has been a television and radio host for more than 40 years, has authored 30 publications, and has books translated into 7 languages. As President and Founder of Revival Fellowship International, John, and his wife Rebecca, have many spiritual sons and daughters in 13 states and 5 countries. John carries and imparts an Elijah Anointing to prepare the Church for discipling nations as mature sons and daughters. John serves on the Council of Elders for the International Coalition of Apostolic Leaders and is a former United States Marine, being a veteran of the Vietnam War. John and Rebecca have been married 47 years, with 4 children and 9 grandchildren.

MORE BOOKS BY JOHN POLIS

Apostolic Functions:
9 Things Apostles Do.

Built Strong:
31 Keys To Spiritual Power.

God Fathers:
How You Can Be One.

Stronger Than Satan:
Understanding Your Authority In Christ.

Victorious:
How To Face, Fight, and Finish Your Battles.

Release The River Within You:
Increasing The Anointing Flow

Put On Your Gloves:
The Five Battles Every Christian Must Win.

Apostolic Advice:
Proven Wisdom for Building Strong Foundations in the Local Church.

Recycled Believers:
Solving The Mystery of Migrating Sheep.

How To Produce Abundance In Your Life:
The Kingdom Secrets Jesus Taught His Disciples.

Biblical Headship:
Making Sense of Submission To Authority.

The Master Builder:
Wisdom for Today's Apostles

Take My Yoke Upon You:
Fulfilling Your 3 Dimensional Destiny

The Kings Are Coming:
Understanding The Kingly Anointing

BE STRONG IN THE LORD:
DISCIPLESHIP SERIES BOOKS BY JOHN POLIS

Living Unshakeable In A Shaking World:
6 Principles For Successful Kingdom Living.

Total Victory Is For You:
5 Smooth Stones To Slay Your Giants.

The Love Of God

How To Obtain Strong Faith

Spiritual Warfare:
No Place For Satan

For these and additional resources to help you in your spiritual growth, go to www.johnpolis.com.

www.ingramcontent.com/pod-product-compliance
Lightning Source LLC
LaVergne TN
LVHW020651100826
845148LV00012B/2426
9781737723653